A D...
EC...

24 HOURS ON A CORAL REEF

VIRGINIA SCHOMP

Cavendish
Square

New York

Published in 2014 by Cavendish Square Publishing, LLC
303 Park Avenue South, Suite 1247, New York, NY 10010

Library of Congress Cataloging-in-Publication Data
Schomp, Virginia.
24 hours on a coral reef / Virginia Schomp.
p. cm. — (a day in an ecosystem)
Includes bibliographical references and index.
Summary: "Take a look at what takes place within a 24-hour period on a coral reef. Learn firsthand about the features, plant life, and animals of the habitat"—Provided by publisher.
ISBN 978-1-60870-892-5 (hardcover) ISBN 978-1-62712-065-4 (paperback)
ISBN 978-1-60870-899-4 (ebook)
1. Coral reef ecology—Juvenile literature. I. Title. II. Title: Twenty four hours on a coral reef.
QH541.5.C7S363 2013
577.7'89—dc23
2011041775

Editor: Peter Mavrikis
Art Director: Anahid Hamparian
Series Designer: Kay Petronio
Photo research by Alison Morretta

Printed in the United States of America

CONTENTS

DAWN

FEEL the warm salty breeze. Wiggle your toes in the cool white sand. You are just in time to watch the sun rise over the Coral Sea. Islands stick their heads above the gentle waves. Closer to shore, you can see dark patches in the clear blue-green water. These are signs of an amazing world beneath the sea—the world of the **coral reef**.

Coral reefs are rocklike formations made by small sea creatures called **corals**. They are found in warm ocean waters all around the world. They cover just one percent of the seafloor, but they are home to 25 percent of all ocean life. The only **ecosystem** with more kinds of plants and animals is the tropical rain forest. That is why coral reefs are sometimes called the "rain forests of the sea."

There are three main types of coral reefs. **Atoll reefs** grow in a ring around a body of shallow water called a lagoon. They may form when a volcano that is surrounded by a reef sinks under the sea. **Fringing reefs**

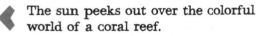

The sun peeks out over the colorful world of a coral reef.

grow along coastlines. They may be attached to the land or separated by a narrow lagoon. **Barrier reefs** form along coastlines, too. But these reefs are farther out to sea. A large lagoon lies between the barrier reef and the shore.

A barrier reef and a blue lagoon surround an island in the Pacific Ocean.

Today, you are visiting the Great Barrier Reef. This giant reef stretches more than 1,250 miles (2,000 kilometers) along the northeast coast of Australia. Thousands of plant and animal **species** live here. Hundreds of new creatures are found every year. You might come across a kind of coral that no one has ever seen before. You might discover a giant fish with razor-sharp teeth or a tiny shrimp that lives between two grains of sand.

So take a deep breath. A world of weird and wonderful creatures is waiting. To explore that world, you must dive down into the ocean. Forget your diving gear. You will not need your mask or air tank. For this adventure, all you need to bring is your imagination.

A space photo of the Great Barrier Reef

THE WORLD'S BIGGEST REEF

The Great Barrier Reef is the world's largest coral reef system. It is made up of about three thousand separate reefs and nine hundred islands. It is so big that it can even be seen from space. American astronaut Douglas Wheelock said it looked like "an explosion of color, motion, and life."

MORNING

DIVE into the water and swim out over the sandy seafloor. Soon you will come to a magical world teeming with life. Mounds of corals sparkle like jewels. Feathery sea fans sway in the currents. Colorful fish dart in and out of the coral reef.

It is hard to believe that this watery kingdom started with one little animal. A single coral animal is called a **polyp**. Coral polyps are soft-bodied sea creatures related to jellyfish. Most polyps measure less than 1 inch (2.5 centimeters) across.

How does such a small creature build such a big reef? It creates a lot of helpers! First, a young polyp attaches itself to a hard surface under the water. Then it divides itself in half to become two polyps. The two become four. Four become eight. In time, there are thousands of polyps.

As each polyp grows, it forms a hard skeleton around its body. A polyp and its skeleton are called a coral. All the corals attach themselves together

◀ The morning light filters down to a mound of coral built by thousands of tiny coral polyps.

Orange coral polyps

A ROCKY HOME

How does a coral make its own skeleton? It sucks up calcium from the seawater. It uses the calcium to make a hard rock called limestone. The limestone skeleton becomes the coral's home. It protects the animal's soft body the same way a shell protects a clam.

to form a coral colony. When the corals die, they leave their skeletons behind. New colonies grow on top of the old ones. Over many years, the layers build up to form the coral reef.

You swim over a mound of coral that looks like a giant brain. Next you see a tall coral with branches like the antlers on a stag, or deer. Hundreds of different types of corals live in the Great Barrier Reef. Each species makes its own kind of colony. Brain coral, staghorn coral, tabletop coral, trumpet coral—can you guess the shape of the reefs from the names of their builders?

Corals that build reefs are known as hard corals. There are also many soft corals growing on the reef. Soft corals do not have hard outer skeletons. Instead, they have a bendable skeleton inside their bodies.

Just like hard corals, soft corals live together in colonies. These colonies look like colorful plants or trees. The names of the corals give a clue to their shape. Sea fans wave back and forth in the currents. Carnation corals show off their "flowers." Cauliflower corals look almost good enough to eat.

Corals are animals, and animals need to eat. How do these little creatures get their food?

All hard corals have tiny plants called **algae** living inside their bodies. Algae live inside some soft corals, too. Like all plants, algae use the energy from sunlight to make their own food. They share the food with their coral partners. Algae also make oxygen, which helps corals live and grow. The tiny plants do one other big job. The skeletons that corals make are white. It is the algae inside the corals that give the reef its rainbow colors.

What do algae get in return for all their gifts? The corals give them a safe and sunny place to live. Corals also give off gases when they eat. These waste products help the algae turn sunlight into food.

These flat mounds were made by colonies of tabletop corals.

Green algae inside living corals

A LIVING GLUE

The little algae that live inside corals have a big name. They are called zooxanthellae (zoh-uh-zan-THE-luh). Another important type of algae on the coral reef is coralline (KOR-uh-line). Coralline algae act like glue. They bind all the different coral colonies together to make one solid reef.

Corals add to their diet by catching food. Every coral polyp has a mouth at the top. The mouth is surrounded by stinging tentacles. Corals use their tentacles to catch tiny animals called **zooplankton**. At night, millions of plankton drift in the seawater. The corals stretch out their tentacles, zap the floating feast, and stuff the plankton into their mouths.

Are you enjoying the warm water? So are the corals! Hard corals grow best at temperatures above 68 degrees Fahrenheit (20 degrees Celsius). They can live in colder water, but they will not form the strong skeletons needed to build reefs. That is why most coral reefs are found in **tropical** oceans.

Hungry coral polyps stretch out their long, stinging tentacles.

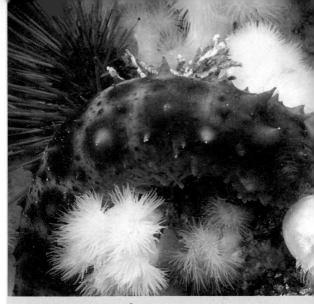

A sea cucumber

Corals are picky in other ways, too. They can only live in saltwater. The water must be shallow and clear. If the water is too deep or cloudy, the algae inside the corals cannot get enough sunlight.

The animals that live on the coral reef help keep the water clear. Sponges and clams are **filter feeders**. They filter seawater through their bodies. They eat the bits of floating food and return clean water to the ocean.

Other creatures clean up the sea bottom. The sea cucumber may look like a walking pickle, but it is really a tough-skinned animal. It crawls over the seafloor, sucking in sand littered with fish poop and parts of dead plants and animals. Yummy! The sea cucumber gobbles up the wastes and spits out cleaned-up sand.

CUCUMBER CLEANERS

Sea cucumbers help keep the ocean floor clean. How good a job do these cleaning crews do? Scientists studied a patch of reef about .6 mile (1 kilometer) long. They measured how much sand the sea cucumbers cleaned in a year. The total came to more than 1,000 tons (1,100 metric tons). That is enough sand to fill about seventy-five dump trucks!

AFTERNOON

COLORFUL fish glide through the water. When you swim near, they swirl around you like confetti. Thousands of other fish dart in and out of every nook in the coral reef.

Fish share their watery home with creatures of all shapes, sizes, and colors. You can see starfish and **sea anemones** clinging to the reef. Tiny shrimps and crabs creep along the coral branches. A sea sponge sprouts from a crack. A giant clam burrows into the sea bottom. Sea horses and turtles graze among the sea grasses.

Why are coral reefs so full of life? When corals build homes for themselves, they also create many living places for other animals. Sea creatures use every inch of this undersea housing complex. Some animals spend their whole lives inside one coral "apartment." Some flit from one part of the reef to another. There are animals that live in the grasses or sand. Others make their home inside sponges. One researcher examined

◀ Blue-lined snapper and many other brightly colored sea creatures make their home on the coral reef.

a large sponge called a loggerhead. He found more than 16,000 shrimps living there!

An animal's special place in the coral reef is called its **niche**. A niche is more than just a living space. It is also the way the animal lives there. Some creatures feed during the daytime. Others come out at night. Each animal eats a particular kind of food. All these different ways of life make it possible for many different species to share the coral reef.

A striped butterflyfish nibbles on corals. Blue and yellow angelfish tear chunks from a sponge. A moray eel pokes its head out from a hole in the reef. Be careful! This sharp-toothed **predator** is looking for lunch. You do not want it to mistake your fingers for a juicy fish!

All these creatures have **adaptations** that help them survive on the coral reef. The moray's long, narrow body is perfect for slinking through holes. Its sharp teeth slant backward to keep its **prey** from wriggling free.

The parrotfish has a birdlike beak for scraping algae from the coral reef.

Butterflyfish and angelfish have flattened bodies. That makes it easy to swim among the coral branches. Other adaptations help these fish eat their favorite foods. The butterflyfish uses its long, pointed mouth to pluck polyps from the reef. Angelfish have overlapping teeth for cutting through tough sponges. They coat each bite with thick mucus. That protects their stomachs from the sharp spines and poisons in sponge bodies.

A moray eel lurks in a hole in the reef, waiting for a meal to swim by.

Adaptations can also help reef animals stay safe from their enemies. Some fish are armed with sharp teeth or spines. Many others live in large groups called schools. In a school, there are always lots of eyes looking out for danger. When a predator attacks, the school explodes. Up, down, right, left, backward! All the fish move together. It is hard for a hunter to pick out one victim from the mass of swift, silvery swimmers.

It is easy to see the fish that crowd this coral city. You may have to look harder to spot some of their roommates. These reef residents include

A curvy sea horse

SNACK ATTACK!

Why does a sea horse look like a horse? So it can grab a quick snack! This strange-looking fish hangs around near the seafloor. It waits for a shrimp to float by. In a flash, the sea horse strikes. With a straight neck, it might miss. Its curved shape is an adaptation that helps it reach just far enough to catch its prey.

an amazing variety of **invertebrates**. Some invertebrates hide in the sand or inside corals. Some look so strange that you might not think they are animals at all.

The Christmas tree worm looks like a pair of small, colorful trees. This sea worm spends its entire life in a hole hollowed out in the reef. The "trees" are its **gills**. They stick out in the water, helping the worm breathe and eat. When danger threatens, the worm pulls in its gills and slams a lid over its hole.

Worms are not the only creatures that make holes in the reef. Small clams, crabs, and scallops also burrow into the corals. Sponges may use acids to dig out their living chambers. Parrotfish chew on the brown and green algae that grow over parts of the reef. Prickly sea urchins graze on the algae, too. As these algae eaters "mow the lawn," they make grooves and tunnels in the reef.

All these actions damage parts of the coral reef. At the same time, they are good for the reef ecosystem. Algae eaters keep the algae from growing too tall and blocking the light. The hole that a worm or clam makes can become shelter for some other animal. When parts of a damaged reef break away, the living corals float to a new place on the seafloor. There they may take hold and start a new coral colony.

The Christmas tree worm can use its gills to filter tiny bits of food from the water.

What does an algae-eating sea urchin have in common with a sea cucumber crawling on the ocean floor? Both of these animals are **echinoderms**. Echinoderms are a group of spiny-skinned sea animals. The most famous member of this group is the sea star, or starfish.

Starfish have no mouths. How do they eat? They push their stomachs out of their bodies. The stomach oozes into the shell of a clam or an oyster. It slurps up the meal. Then the starfish sucks its stomach back in.

Here comes a hungry sea snail. It bites off the starfish's arm. No problem! This prickly animal has an amazing way of saving itself from predators. It can crawl away and grow a new arm. Even if only one arm is left, the wounded animal may drag itself to safety and grow a whole new body.

Echinoderms move very slowly on rows of tiny tube feet. The feet look like tubes with suction cups on the end. Seawater circulates in the animal's body. When the water is sucked out of the feet, they stick to the reef. When water flows into the feet, the suction cups come loose and the animal can move.

The stonefish's colors and lumpy shape blend in with the seafloor.

A yellow butterflyfish chomps on algae. A bright blue starfish clings to a mound of coral. **Nudibranchs** crawl along the sea bottom. These little soft-bodied animals are related to the snails you might find in your garden. But nudibranchs come in so many dazzling colors that they are often called the "jewels of the sea."

Why is the world of the coral reef so colorful? Some fish use color to call attention to themselves. That can keep another fish from wandering into their favorite burrow or feeding spot. Colors and markings also help fish recognize members of their own species.

Other reef animals use color as **camouflage**. The shells of cowries are the same color as the soft coral they live on. That helps these small snails hide from predators. The bumpy brown stonefish looks like a rock lying on the seafloor. That makes it easier for this hunter to catch its prey.

Color can also be a warning. Nudibranchs have nasty chemicals and stingers in their bodies. Their poster colors are a message to predators: DANGER! DO NOT EAT! The surgeonfish has a sharp spine at the base of its tail. This fish would rather eat than fight, so it uses color to point out its weapon.

Color can even be a trick. The butterflyfish has a spot of color near its tail. The spot looks like a giant eye. That eyespot can confuse a predator just long enough for the fish to make its escape.

A well-dressed decorator crab

A CRAFTY CRAB

Is that a rock crawling on the seafloor? Look again! It just might be a decorator crab. This little crab is a master of disguise. It sticks bits of algae and sponges all over its shell. You might not even notice the camouflaged crab until it takes its living decorations for a walk.

EVENING

THE SUN is sinking low in the sky. The waters begin to darken. Some animals tuck themselves into sheltered areas to rest. Others are just waking up. These **nocturnal** animals rest during the day and come out to feed at night.

Turn on your waterproof flashlight. Suddenly you are floating inside a cloud of wriggling creatures. The zooplankton are rising up from the seafloor. They will spend the night feeding on other tiny animals and plants in the water.

Many of the plankton will become food for other animals. Coral polyps stretch out their tentacles to snare the little swimmers. Basket stars unfurl their arms to comb food from the water. Schools of pink squirrelfish and cardinalfish also snack on plankton. These small fish have big eyes to help them find their prey in the dark.

Larger predators visit the outer edge of the reef. Whale sharks and

◀ The sun sets over an undersea garden of corals.

Smaller fish have nothing to fear from this filter-feeding whale shark.

manta rays look scary, but they are no threat to people. These huge fish are filter feeders. They have cruised in from deeper parts of the ocean to strain plankton from the seawater.

Watch out for that tiger shark! This nocturnal hunter eats fish, crabs, turtles, and just about anything else that moves. One tiger shark even ate a "reef cam." Scientists had set up the big camera under the water to film the animals of the Great Barrier Reef.

Shine your light over the seafloor. Many **mollusks** make their home here. Mollusks are soft-bodied invertebrates. They often have a hard outer shell for protection. Clams, oysters, and snails are all mollusks. Mollusks without shells include nudibranchs, squid, and octopuses.

A clam can hide inside its shell. How do shell-less mollusks protect themselves? Nudibranchs use their poisons and stingers. Many octopuses and squid have their own secret weapons.

Do you see that octopus crawling along the sand? Uh-oh! So does the tiger shark! As the shark attacks, the octopus squirts a cloud of black ink into the water. The ink confuses the shark for a few seconds. That is just enough time for the octopus to escape through a crack in the reef.

You will also find lots of **crustaceans** on the sea bottom. Crustaceans are named for their "crusty" outer shell. These weird-looking creatures include many species of crabs, shrimps, and lobsters.

During the day, most crustaceans rest in cracks in the reef. All you can see are their long antennas sticking out. At night, they scurry out from their hiding places to search for food. Some crustaceans eat plants. Others eat animals. Still others feed on just about anything they can find.

A crustacean's shell gives it some protection from predators. A few kinds of crabs go a step farther. They carry around their own bodyguards!

A boxer crab scuttles across the seafloor. The little crab is holding a sea anemone in each of its

A deadly blue-ringed octopus

BEAUTIFUL BUT DEADLY

The blue-ringed octopus is dull gray or brown. When it feels threatened, bright blue rings appear all over its body. The color is a warning. This octopus produces one of the world's deadliest poisons. One bite from its sharp beak can kill a person in just a few minutes.

A boxer crab waves its secret weapon, two stinging sea anemones.

claws. Sea anemones are close relatives of coral polyps. Their tentacles are loaded with stingers. When an enemy gets too close, the crab sticks out its anemones just like a boxer holding up his fists. The message is clear: BACK OFF OR ELSE!

Why would a sea anemone help a crab scare off its enemies? It gets a free meal in return. As the anemone rides around on the crab, it comes across more food than it could find on its own.

Other animals also team up to help each other survive on the coral reef. The goby fish needs a place to live and hide. The alpheid (AL-fee-ud) shrimp is nearly blind, so it has trouble watching out for predators. These two little creatures share a burrow in the sand. The shrimp digs the hole and keeps it clean. The goby stands guard. When it sees a meat-eating fish, it warns the shrimp by shaking its tail. If the hunter gets too close, the goby dives headfirst into the hole.

The banded coral shrimp has a different way of helping its partners. This shrimp is a "cleaner." It sits in front of a crack in the reef and waits for some large fish to appear. The fish have not come to eat the shrimp. Instead, they line up and wait their turn. The shrimp crawls all over its "clients,"

A colorful giant clam

CORAL REEF GIANTS

Giant clams can grow more than 4 feet (1.2 meters) long. That makes them the world's largest clams. Like corals, these big mollusks have two ways of eating. They filter plankton from the water. They also get food from algae living inside their bodies. The algae give giant clams their bright, beautiful colors.

An angelfish gets a checkup from a cleaner shrimp.

removing tiny **parasites** from their skin, mouth, and gills. The cleaner shrimp gets a meal. The client fish get rid of parasites that could make them sick.

The banded coral shrimp has red and white stripes to attract clients to its cleaning station. Other types of cleaner shrimp and fish also use color to advertise their services. Some cleaners even do a special "dance" to tell customers they are open for business.

But advertisements are not always truthful. The false cleaner fish looks just like a real cleaner fish called a wrasse (ras). It has the same colors as the wrasse. It even does the same dance. That helps this trickster grab a quick snack. The false cleaner swims up to a big meat-eating fish. Instead of cleaning off parasites, it takes a bite out of the fish's tail. Then it races away before the predator can bite back.

A clownfish in the tentacles of a sea anemone

A LIVING HOME

The clownfish and sea anemone are partners. The fish is covered with mucus that protects it from the anemone's sting. That lets it live among the tentacles, where it is safe from most predators. How does the clownfish say "thank you"? It drives off any fish that try to take a bite out of its anemone home.

NIGHT

ARE YOU ready to take a break from the water? Why not visit one of the islands in the Great Barrier Reef? Some are **continental islands**. These bodies of land were once part of the coastline. Thousands of years ago, they became surrounded by water. There are also many small, low islands called **cays**. Cays are formed from piles of dead coral ground into sand and rock by the waves.

Some cays are bare. Others have low shrubs or trees. There are even coral islands covered with dense green forests. All these environments provide a home for hundreds of different kinds of birds. You might see dull black noddies and brightly colored parrots and kingfishers. Little finches grow no bigger than your hand. Flightless birds called southern cassowaries can grow as tall as a basketball player.

Some of these birds live on the reef islands all year round. Others spend most of their time in lands up north. When winter comes, they fly

◀ After sundown, the green turtle may sleep in the shelter of a rock or reef.

In the winter, black noddies raise their young on the islands of the Great Barrier Reef.

down to the warmth of the Great Barrier Reef. They feast on the fish and shellfish. They build nests and raise their chicks. Sometimes the parents or baby birds become food for other coral reef creatures. That give-and-take makes birds an important part of the reef ecosystem.

You dry off on a sandy beach. Beyond the white sands is a dark tangle of ferns, vines, shrubs, and trees. Crickets and tree frogs sing in the darkness. A snake called a death adder is coiled up in a tree hollow. A brown tree snake creeps over the forest floor, hunting for rats and lizards.

The adder and tree snake spend nearly all their time on land. Sea snakes are at home both on land and in the water. The banded sea snake lays its eggs in mounds of sand on the beach. At night, it swims in the shallow waters around the reef. The snake uses its flat tail like a paddle as it searches for fish, crabs, and other sea creatures.

Sea turtles also divide their time between the land and water. Male turtles may come ashore to find a mate. The rest of the time, you will see them swimming around the reef, munching on sea grass, sponges, and shellfish.

Female sea turtles must leave the water to lay their eggs. A female turtle may swim hundreds of miles to return to the beach where she was born. She comes back to her nesting beach every few years.

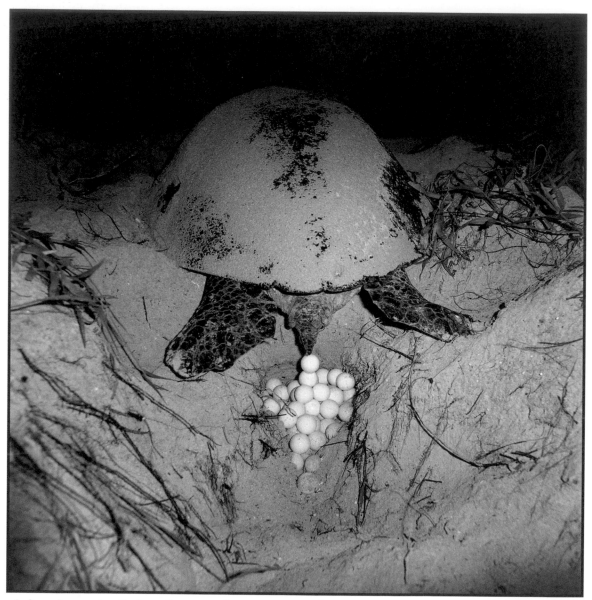

A female sea turtle lays her eggs in a warm, moist nest on the beach.

She may lay thousands of eggs in her lifetime. But her babies face danger from the minute they hatch. Hungry predators wait on the sand and in the water. Only a few of the mother's hatchlings will grow up into adult turtles.

Another flashlight is shining. Follow the light, and you will meet other visitors to the coral island. A small group of scientists have come to study hawksbill turtles. These sea turtles are an **endangered species**. People have killed them for their meat and their beautiful shells. They have robbed turtle eggs from the nests. They have taken over many of the nesting beaches.

It is nesting season now. A female hawksbill is dragging her heavy body up the cool, dark beach. She uses her flippers to scoop out a nest in the sand. She lays more than one hundred eggs that look just like ping-pong balls. The turtle covers her eggs with sand. She is ready to return to the water.

Baby sea turtles

RACING TURTLES

Baby sea turtles are on their own when they hatch. They wait for the sun to set. Then they burst out of their nest and scurry down the beach. Hungry birds, crabs, and other predators try to catch them. Out of one hundred hatchlings, only one or two may make it to the water.

But before the mother turtle leaves the beach, the scientists attach metal tags to her flippers. The number on the tags will let researchers recognize this turtle the next time she is found. They will be able to keep track of where she travels. They will find out how often she visits her nesting beach. Learning more about hawksbills will help them find ways to save these important reef creatures.

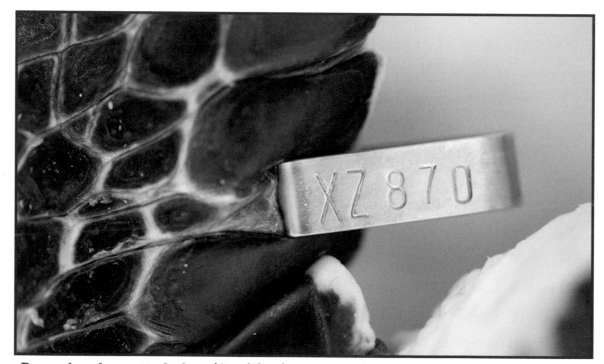

Researchers have attached an identification tag to this sea turtle flipper.

Hawksbill turtles are not the only endangered reef creatures. Many other species are in trouble, too. In fact, whole coral reefs are in danger of disappearing forever.

Natural forces such as storms can damage reefs. But most of the problems are caused by people. Large fishing boats may catch too many fish. Overfishing upsets the balance of life on the coral reef. Some fishermen use harmful fishing methods. They drag huge nets across the seafloor. They blast reefs with dynamite or sprinkle poison in the water. All these practices hurt reefs and reef creatures.

Water pollution also damages reefs. When people clear land along the coast, soil washes into the ocean. Chemicals and other wastes run off from farms and cities.

Even a fun day at the beach can cause trouble for coral reefs. Swimmers may leave trash that ends up in the water. They may damage reefs by walking on them or breaking off pieces of coral.

The greatest threat to coral reefs comes from **global warming**. Earth's temperature is slowly rising. Most scientists believe that this is caused by human activities such as burning coal and oil. When the ocean waters get too warm, coral polyps eject the algae that live inside them. Without their algae, the corals turn white. Scientists call this **coral bleaching**. Large sections of bleached corals can die because they no longer have algae to make food for them.

The pale color of bleached corals is a sign of trouble on the coral reef.

When coral reefs die, reef creatures lose their homes. People suffer, too. Reefs help protect our coastlines from storms. The fish and shellfish provide food for many people. People also depend on coral reefs for jobs. Some make a living from fishing. Some work in hotels and other businesses that serve tourists. Every year, millions of people come to relax on reef beaches and swim in the clear reef waters.

You have met some scientists who are studying sea turtles. Other people are learning about other parts of the reef. How do the animals work together to keep the ecosystem healthy? How do human actions affect reefs? The answers to these questions can help governments protect their coral reefs.

Today, you explored the largest protected sea area in the world. The Great Barrier Reef Marine Park was created by the government

A prickly crown-of-thorns starfish

A DANGEROUS STAR

The crown-of-thorns sea star is a natural part of the reef ecosystem. The starfish eats corals. Other animals eat the starfish. But in recent years, the crown-of-thorns population has soared. Hungry starfish have wiped out entire reefs. No one knows why this is happening. Some scientists think the starfish may be thriving on farm fertilizers that wash into the water.

A golden damsel

A BALANCING ACT

How does overfishing upset the balance of life on the coral reef? Just ask the damselfish! This little fish is a farmer. It kills corals to make room for its algae gardens. Grouper fish keep the damsels under control. But sometimes, fishermen take too many groupers. Then damselfish fill the waters and algae take over the reef.

of Australia. Park managers watch over the reef and the land and waters around it. They make sure everyone follows strict rules on fishing and other activities. The rules let visitors enjoy the reef without harming it.

Other governments around the world are also taking action. They have set up their own sea parks. They are working to clean up their air and water. They are trying to fight global warming by reducing their use of coal and oil. They are asking all of us to help take care of coral reefs.

The first light of day touches the water. You follow a sea turtle as she dives back under the surface. Coral polyps are pulling in their tentacles. Nocturnal animals are settling down, while daytime feeders are waking. You can see bright blue parrotfish peeking out of holes in the reef. They dart out into the "rush hour." Their nooks are not empty for long. Big-eyed squirrelfish and cardinalfish duck into the shadows to sleep away the daylight hours.

You swim by a patch of corals that look like white finger bones. The bleached corals are a sign that this reef is in trouble. But scientists tell us that even badly damaged coral reefs can recover. We must work to protect the reef waters. We must take better care of our planet. That way, this beautiful city under the sea will see many bright, busy mornings.

PROTECTING CORAL REEFS

You do not have to be a scientist to take care of coral reefs. Here are a few ways we can help protect this beautiful and important ecosystem.

- Use less water and energy.
- Clean up trash on the beach.
- Keep your hands and feet away from the coral.
- Do not buy products made from coral or turtle shells.

WHAT ARE CORAL REEFS?

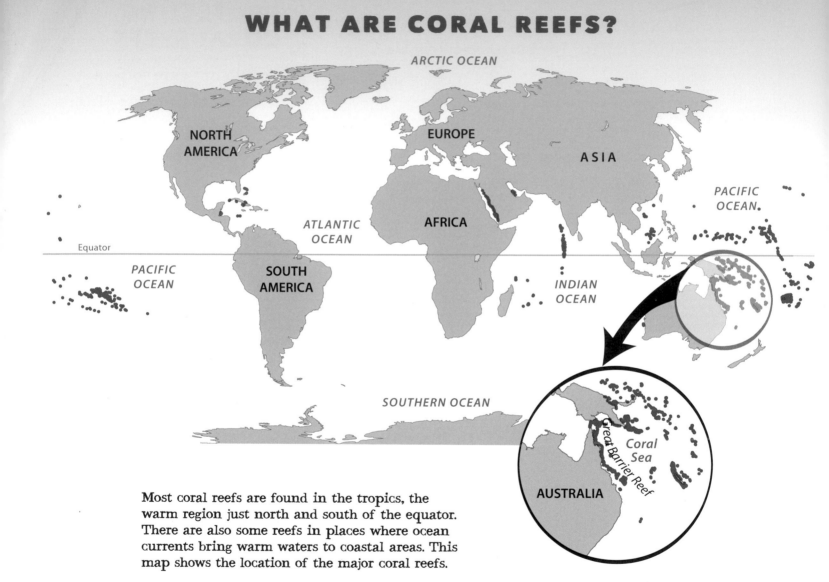

Most coral reefs are found in the tropics, the warm region just north and south of the equator. There are also some reefs in places where ocean currents bring warm waters to coastal areas. This map shows the location of the major coral reefs.

FAST FACTS ABOUT THE GREAT BARRIER REEF

LOCATION: Off the northeast coast of Australia, in the Coral Sea.

SIZE: About 1,250 miles (2,000 kilometers) long. Total area is about 135,000 square miles (350,000 square kilometers).

TEMPERATURES: Water temperatures range from about 72°F (22°C) to 84°F (29°C).

PLANTS: Algae, sea grasses, and tiny floating plants called phytoplankton.

ANIMALS: *Fish* include angelfish, butterflyfish, cardinalfish, clownfish, frogfish, gobies, morays, parrotfish, rays, sea horses, sharks, squirrelfish, stonefish, and surgeonfish. *Echinoderms* include sea cucumbers, sea urchins, and starfish (also called sea stars). *Crustaceans* include crabs, lobsters, scallops, and shrimps. *Mollusks* include clams, nudibranchs, oysters, octopuses, snails, and squid. *Reptiles* include green turtles, hawksbill turtles, leatherback turtles, banded sea snakes, and sea kraits. *Sea mammals* include bottlenose dolphins, dugongs, and humpback whales. There are also many kinds of *corals, sponges, sea worms, sea anemones,* and *jellyfish*.

POPULATION: About 1,025,000 people live in the Great Barrier Reef region. That includes about 69,000 Aboriginal (a-buh-RIH-juh-nul) Australians and Torres Strait Islanders. These two indigenous (native) groups have lived in the region for many thousands of years and are considered the Traditional Owners of the reef.

GLOSSARY

adaptations—Ways in which living things adapt, or change to survive under the conditions in a certain environment.

algae (AL-jee)—Simple plantlike organisms that live mostly in the water.

atoll reefs—Ring-shaped coral reefs surrounding a lagoon.

barrier reefs—Coral reefs that are separated from the coastline by a large lagoon.

camouflage (KAM-uh-flaj)—Coloring or other physical features that help living things blend in with their surroundings, hiding them from other animals.

cays (kayz)—Small, low-lying islands made of sand and coral fragments.

continental islands—Bodies of land that are connected to a continent but are completely surrounded by water.

coral bleaching—A condition in which coral polyps expel their algae, turn white, and often die from lack of food.

coral reef—A rocklike formation found in warm ocean waters, formed from colonies of coral polyps living on top of the skeletons of dead polyps.

corals—Coral polyps and their hard outer skeletons.

crustaceans (krus-TAY-shunz)—Animals that live mostly in the water and have a hard outer skeleton and a body divided into many segments. Lobsters, shrimps, and crabs are crustaceans.

echinoderms (ih-KIE-nuh-dermz)—Sea animals with a five-part body, an outer skeleton of hard plates, and tube feet. Echinoderms include starfish, sea urchins, and sea cucumbers.

ecosystem—An area that is home to a particular group of plants and animals, which are specially suited to living in that environment. An ecosystem includes all the living things of the area plus all the nonliving things, such as the temperature, water, and rocks.

endangered species—Plants and animals that are in danger of becoming extinct, or dying out completely.

filter feeders—Animals that feed by filtering, or straining, tiny particles of food from the surrounding water.

fringing reefs—Coral reefs that form close to the coastline.

gills—A part of a water creature's body that is used mainly for breathing and sometimes for filtering food from the water.

global warming—The rising temperature of planet Earth. Most scientists believe that global warming is caused, at least in part, by human activities such as burning coal and oil, which release gases that trap heat near the planet.

invertebrates (in-VUR-tuh-bruts)—Animals without a backbone, such as worms, insects, and mollusks.

mollusks—Soft-bodied invertebrates that live mostly in the water and usually have a hard shell. Snails, crabs, and octopuses are mollusks.

niche (nitch)—The special habitat of a species. Niche includes the place where the plant or animal lives and the way it survives in that place.

nocturnal—Active mainly at night.

nudibranchs (NOO-duh-branks)—Small colorful mollusks without shells.

parasites—Animals that live in or on another animal's body, using it for food and giving nothing in return.

polyp (PAH-lup)—An individual coral animal. Coral polyps are small tube-shaped invertebrates that are related to jellyfish and sea anemones.

predator—An animal that hunts and kills other animals for food.

prey—An animal that is hunted by a predator.

sea anemones (see uh-NEH-mun-eez)—Sea animals that are related to corals and jellyfish. A sea anemone looks like a large coral polyp without a skeleton.

species (SPEE-sheez)—Specific types of plants and animals.

tropical—Found in the tropics, the warm region just north and south of the earth's equator.

zooplankton (zoh-uh-PLANK-ton)—Masses of very tiny animals that drift in bodies of water.

FIND OUT MORE

Books

Bodden, Valerie. *Great Barrier Reef.* Mankato, MN: Creative Education, 2010.

George, Lynn. *Coral Reef Builders.* New York: Rosen Publishing, 2011.

Green, Jen. *Life in a Coral Reef.* New York: Gareth Stevens, 2010.

McKenzie, Precious. *Coral Reefs.* Vero Beach, FL: Rourke Publishing, 2011.

Wojahn, Rebecca Hogue, and Donald Wojahn. *A Coral Reef Food Chain.*
  Minneapolis: Lerner Publications, 2010.

Websites

About Coral Reefs

www.coral.org/resources

This site from the Coral Reef Alliance has lots of information about coral reefs. Click on "Photobank" for thousands of photos of reefs and the creatures that depend on them.

Biomes-Habitats: Coral Reef Animal Printouts

www.enchantedlearning.com/biomes/coralreef/coralreef.shtml

This Enchanted Learning site has printable pictures and activity sheets for learning about the animals of the coral reef.

Biomes of the World: Tropical Oceans

www.mbgnet.net/salt/coral/indexfr.htm

Follow the links for information and photos relating to coral reefs and the animals that live there. This colorful site is presented by the Missouri Botanical Garden.

Great Barrier Reef

http://video.nationalgeographic.com/video/player/places/parks-and-nature-places/oceans/oceans-barrier-reef.html

The four-minute video at this National Geographic site gives you a close-up look at the Great Barrier Reef.

INDEX

Page numbers in **boldface** are illustrations.

ABOUT THE AUTHOR

VIRGINIA SCHOMP has written more than eighty books for young readers on topics including dinosaurs, dolphins, world history, American history, myths, and legends. She lives among the tall pines of New York's Catskill Mountain region. When she is not writing books, she enjoys hiking, gardening, baking (and eating!) cookies, watching old movies and new anime, and, of course, reading, reading, and reading.

PHOTO CREDITS

The photographs in this book are used by permission and through the courtesy of:

Front cover: Mark Conlin/Alamy.

Alamy: Ulla Lohmann/LOOK Die Bildagentur der Fotografen GmbH, 17; cbimages, 18; Reinhard Dirscherl, 20; David Fleetham, 25; Georgette Douwma/ImageState, 40. *Getty Images:* Jeff Hunter, 1; Oxford Scientific, 12 (left); Max Gibbs, 16; DEA/P. Jaccod/De Agostini, 34; Joel Sartore, 36. *The Image Works:* Dr. David Wachenfeld/Auscape, 38. *Superstock:* NHPA, 4, 11, 32; Minden Pictures, 6, 10, 12 (right), 19, 22, 29, 39; Science Faction, 7, 14, 26, 30; Eye Ubiquitous, 8; All Canada Photos, 13; Robert Harding Picture Library, 21; NaturePL, 24; age fotostock, 27; Animals Animals, 28, 35.